HOW TO STAY
MARRIED!

HOW TO STAY MARRIED!

A WEDDING BAND IS A SIMPLE CIRCLE OF METAL THAT
IS REPRESENTATIVE OF THE PROMISE TO LOVE HONOR
AND CHERISH UNTIL DEATH DO YOU PART.

WHAT GOD HAS JOINED TOGETHER
LET NO MAN PUT ASUNDER!

SANDRA WILSON

Library of Congress Control Number:		2015913461
ISBN:	Hardcover	978-1-5035-9971-0
	Softcover	978-1-5035-9972-7
	eBook	978-1-5035-9973-4

Rev. date: 11/10/2015

To order additional copies of this book, contact:
Xlibris
1-888-795-4274
www.Xlibris.com
Orders@Xlibris.com
709793

CONTENTS

Acknowledgements.. xi

Introduction.. xiii

Preface xv

   1. Marriage 1

   2. Priority.. 31

   3. The Husband's Role................................... 37

   4. The Wife's Role... 46

   5. Keep the Fire Burning................................ 66

   6. Intimacy... 73

   7. Don't Let the Devil Steal Your Marriage 81

Biography... 89

Marriage Is a Lifelong Commitment!

For Better or Worse, Richer or Poorer!

Sandra Wilson

Let marriage be held in honor among all, and let the marriage bed be undefiled, for God will judge the sexually immoral and adulterous. **(Hebrews 13:4).**

He who finds a wife finds a good thing and obtains favor from the Lord. **(Proverb 18:22).**

Acknowledgements

My deepest appreciation to my Father in Heaven, for making it possible for me to write this book. To my awesome husband Larry, who's truly God sent, for his love and support, for being my inspiration, without him being the husband that God called him to be, it would be impossible for me to write this book. Big thanks to my daughter Adrian, my daughter-in-law Kortney who is my hero, my faith that kept me on this journey, also a big thanks to my family. Thanks to Dr. Pricilla Thomas and Dr. Sandra Chavis. Thanks to my photographer Mickey Rivers. I truly thank God for my mother, the late Mrs. Marian Bowens, who played a great role in my life. My motto is: I can do all things through Christ who strengthens me (Philippians 4:13).

Introduction

Marriage is about keeping a covenant, as Jesus does with his bride, the church. Marriage is God's doing; it was his design in the creation of man as male and female; marriage is for God's Glory. Getting married is one thing, but staying married is *awesome*. In today's society, there are many people who get married but don't know how to stay married. Many people wonder why did I get married? That's why it's so important to pray and wait on the Lord before making this great commitment. It's so important to know how to stay married. There are roles to be played between both the husband and wife. Marriage isn't just a license or a ring; it's a lifelong commitment, investing time; it's work between the both of you. Once you make a vow, it's a covenant to keep until death do you part. Prayer is very vital in a marriage because the enemy (Satan) comes to steal, kill, and destroy what God has joined together. When the Lord joined me and my Boaz together twentynine years ago, our union has been blessed; we have had more good times in this union versus bad times. Why? Because we put Christ first and kept the third party out. It worked for us and I pray that it will work for you. Remember what God has joined together, let no man put asunder.

Preface

How To Stay Married teaches readers how to meet challenges of marriage and to realize that it is a lifelong commitment between two partners. This book is written to help save marriages, to heal and build up broken marriages, to keep marriages healthy and happy, until death do you part. If you apply these rules and truths, your marriage will be blessed. I pray that this book will bless your union. What God joins together, let no man put asunder.

Chapter 1

Marriage

Marriage is the foundation of all society, and so this topic is very important. Explaining marital duties to you is much easier than persuading you to do them. Conform your will to what the scriptures say. The union between a husband and wife is so beautiful because it stands as a picture between Christ and the church. What a beautiful picture: marriage is a covenant, so God is a part of every marriage.

God joins the couple together so their sexual intimacy is not sinful. "What therefore God joined together, let no man put asunder (separate) 'Mark 10:9. "Marriage is honorable in all, and the bed undefiled: but whoremongers and adulterers God will judge," Hebrews 13:4. "A marriage is more than a license, its love, respect, commitment, and submission. Its work between the both of you being as one, marriage is love not lust, there's a different between love and lust. Love is eternal and lust only last for a season.

Genesis 2:24: Therefore shall a man leave his father and his mother, and shall cleave unto his wife: and they shall be one flesh. This scripture do not mean to ignore your parents and not spend any time with them. It's simply saying recognize that your marriage has created a new family and that this new family is a higher priority than your previous family. "Cleave means "to stick to, or join with. God himself means that the both of you will be joined together in Holy Matrimony. "Leave and cleave" is a bond, and it's also a beautiful picture of the union God intended it to be.

God's ideal plan for marriage is one man for one woman for one lifetime. God's pattern for marital happiness is evident when a man loves and leads his family, with children who obey and reverence their parents (Eph. 6:1-4), with a wife who respects and supports her husband's leadership (Eph. 5:21-33). A mutually supportive attitude must characterize both husband and wife if they are to succeed in building a harmonious home. Marriage is so important in the mind of God that it was the first of three divine institutions and was patterned to illustrate Christ's love for the church.

Getting married is one thing but staying married is awesome. There's a different between a marriage and a wedding, a marriage last until death do you part, a wedding last only for a few minutes. According to God's word, marriage is much more than a "contract";

marriage is a God-made covenant. Once you make a promise to God it cannot be broken. I take thee to be my lawful wedded husband or wife, to have and to hold from this day forward, for better or for worse, for richer or poorer in sickness and in in health; to cherish and to love, and I promise to be faithful to you until death do you part. When you made this vow you made it unto God.

God's word clearly states that it's better not to make a vow unto the Lord and not keep it. Making a promise to God and not keeping it is the work of a fool; such a thing leads to God's anger and judgment. If you really love God, you will keep all of his promises to him, any time you make a promise God don't delay in fulfilling it. He has no pleasures in fools; keep your vow (Ecclesiastes 5:4-7).

Too many couples take marriage vows lightly. Separation should never once be done causally or out of anger, this will cause you to drift farther apart until divorce take place. Divorce is not God's perfect plan for marriage, even if it has become acceptable in the world. The word speaks "Live Joyfully with your wife whom you love all the days of your life which he has given you under the sun – all the days of futility for that is your portion in this life and in your work at which you toil under the sun (Ecclesiastes 9:9).

Getting married is a great decision in your life; make sure you pray and ask God whether or not he or she is the right person that you should marry—that is, if you are not already married. Make sure you pray and wait on the Lord before making this lifelong commitment. Once you have made a vow between you and your spouse, it's a covenant to keep until death do you part. When you put Christ first in your marriage, it will last forever. Prayer is very important because the enemy comes to steal, kill, and destroy what God has joined together; thus, you both have to stay prayed up.

Marriage is never about me, myself, and I. It's about us, ours; it's about lifetime commitment, of becoming one. Marriage is about being a helper to one another; it's about establishing a family.

- Be honest! Be truthful! Be open because once you share your faults with one another, this causes your marriage to flow a lot easier and your marriage will be better off.
- Love covers a multitude of feelings and emotions. Becoming one results in a stronger marriage, less hurt, more respect, and less problems because of a willingness to bring closer together. True love brings comfort into the marriage.
- First and foremost, it is very important that you put Christ first in your marriage. Without him being the center of our marriage and our unwillingness to rely on him, who gives us the power and love and strength and wisdom and endurance, we are not able to fulfill Mark 10:9 which says what God has joined together, let no man put asunder.
- Let us never stop enjoying one another. Marriage is a great gift from God to be enjoyed. Enjoy the little things in life with your spouse. Keeping love alive keeps your marriage alive!

Think back on the day when you married the both of you looked deeply in each other's eyes with a love to be cherished; then you made a covenant to God that until death do you part regardless of the circumstances. That moment, you made that promise to God and believed what you said at the time you said it. It seemed so simple when you spoke those powerful words. So much love was streaming from your heart that you knew that you would not let anything separate that binding promise you both made on your awesome day.

Marriage is an awesome thing joined and ordained by God, then both of you become one flesh. It's no more *me, myself,* and *I.* It's now *us, we, ours*; your body becomes his, and his body becomes yours. It's no more *my* decision but it's *our* decision that we both make together. It's not enough to be married but to be in love. During these thirty-five blessed years, my husband and I are still deeply in love. Our love has grown stronger as the years have gone by.

I don't care what anybody says about love growing old. After being in a marriage for a long period of time, that's a lie from the pits of hell. It keeps getting better and better with time. We enjoy each other, my husband is my best friend, my lover, my inspiration, and he's my king. I'm his best friend, his lover, and his inspiration, and I'm his queen. He's always there for me and I'm always there for my Boaz.

I'm proud to say, during these thirty five years, I've always been faithful to my husband. Not one time had I had a desire to cheat on him or to leave him, and he's always been faithful to me. I'm thankful that the Lord has preserved our union. The Lord couldn't have given me a greater husband. All I can say that the love we have for each other keeps getting better.

Marriage is one of the most important choices you will ever have to make in life. The choice you make will determine if you will have a happy marriage or an unhappy marriage. Marriage is a covenant made

- before God
- to each other
- in the eyes of society
- according to the laws of the land

God says that he witnesses the covenant that a couple makes when they get married. The Lord has been a witness between you and the wife of your youth, (who) is your companion and your wife by covenant (Malachi 2:14). A covenant is a contract, which is agreed upon by two parties. It is a commitment that has a beginning point and consequences for breaking it.

It is important to pray and ask God to help you choose the best person for you, the one most suited to your needs and according to God's plan. Then it is important to obey God's will. This means you will choose to be where God wants you to be. Marriage is a spiritual training program designed by God. It takes his strength and love to live out a lifetime with another fallen human being. We were never meant to be able to do it on our own.

When you are distressed, go to another room if you can and get down on your knees and pour out your hurts and frustrations to the Lord. Open your Bible and find comfort or uplifting passages to read. Sing a praise song to the Lord in heart. Battle (if necessary) through the rough times, hold on through the tough times and be happy during the good times. Remember to always pray for one another.

Marriage is not meant to end in divorce. Marriage is meant to be a partnership wherein two people work together in life. There are many things married couples can do to help strengthen their marriages. No two marriages are identical. What works for one couple may cause strife for another. Remember to base your marriage on the word of God. There are so many people in today's society who marry for the wrong reasons—some marry to be free from parents, to have sex, just because a person has a good job, or because of their status and rank.

There are many who marry just because they have friends that are married. There are so many wrong reasons why people get married and end up in a divorce court. You should wait on the Lord because he knows the right time and who the right person is. If it's the right person, then you will have no problem loving each other. Have a willingness to be there for one another, while each of you try to fulfill one another's dreams. Why marry if you don't want to commit to that person. You shouldn't marry just to say that I am married. Marriage is a lifelong commitment.

When making your wedding vows, it's unto the Lord. God has made somebody just for you. If you are seeking God first in your life, then it will be impossible for you to miss the person whom God has for you. God has a time and season for everything. It's possible to find the right person but marry at the wrong time. If you rush into marriage too quickly, it could bring trouble into the marriage that you could have avoided if you had waited. Good things come to those who wait. Many people miss what God has for them when they turn to their own ways. Sometimes one person tries to push the other person into marriage. Warning! Warning! If this is happening, the best thing to do is back off. Either the person is not the right person, the timing is wrong, or somebody's mind is not convinced.

Marriage is a decision where both parties freely commit themselves to each other. If two people can't be in agreement about whether or not to marry, then how will they ever be in agreement concerning the thousands of decisions they will make after they are married? Amos 3:3 "Can two walk together, except they are in agreement?" If you don't know for sure whether to marry a person, then don't do it.

Marriage should always bring a happy anticipation and assurance, not a fearful questioning of whether or not the marriage will make it. While you are waiting for God to bring your future spouse to you, make sure you are preparing yourself to be the kind of spouse you want your mate to be.

Real marriage is not something that just happens; it's a deep communion between two souls who find completion in each other; it's ordained by God. True marriage is to be entered with respect and love and full of understanding of its significance to be completed. Marriage has to be spiritual and joined together by God. When it is spiritual in thoughts, purpose, and action, it becomes oneness; it becomes peaceful, and a happy union. In a marriage, never stop doing the things that brought you together in the first place. Never let the sun go down on your wrath, meaning never go to bed angry with one another, if you had an argument before you go to bed, make sure you ask each other for forgiveness before going to sleep. Whatever you do, never take each other for granted, for what you take for granted may disappear. Whatever you do for your spouse, do it with a great attitude of duty or sacrifice, do it with a spirit of joy and with a willing heart.

Relationships are something that need to be worked on at all times, even when it is broken and needs fixing. Cherish every moment with your spouse, never deny one another. Submit and love one another. A good marriage means never expecting your husband to wear a halo or your wife to have angel wings. It's all about the love that you have for each other. A healthy marriage is all about giving one another an atmosphere in which you both can grow. It's definitely not looking for perfection in each other. It's about having patience, understanding, and a sense of humor. It's not only marrying the right person but it's about *being* the right person.

God has given us separate roles that are equally important but requiring different responsibilities. God created man and woman to be joined together as one, and as one function in the way he outlined it in the Bible. I believe that I was created to be my husband's helpmeet, and that he is the principal figure in our home. I truly accept the role and honor it as a divine appointment from God. Wives, submit yourself to your own husbands as you do to the Lord, for the husband is the head of the house. When you allow the Lord to be Lord over your marriage, it will last until death do you part.

Often in a marriage, the first thing that goes out is the friendship. If you have children(s), you raise them together and you both work around the house together. After being married for a long period of time, things change. Before, you both went out on dates and had fun. But as time passed, you don't do anything for fun anymore. It's like your friendship has gotten stale and has come to an endless to-do list. Studies shows that most couples spend more than thirty minutes a day chatting about nonlogistical issues, most of the talking they do is about who's going to the grocery store, what's for dinner, etc. *That's very dangerous in a marriage*! If you don't feel connected as friends, it's hard to feel connected as lovers.

In a marriage, friendship is the glue that keeps you together. After you marry, life seems to get busy and settle into routines. As friends in a marriage, you should look forward to every moment that you get together. Most people don't realize that friendship in marriage is so important. When you become friends, you want to be with your spouse and spend quality time together. It's important to be friends in marriage. My husband and I are best friends. There's no one who can come between our friendship. During these thirty-five years we've had each other's best interest, he has my back and I got his back. We enjoy being with each other every chance we get.

Friendship brings life to your marriage. It adds stability and strength. Lack of friendship will cause your love to grow cold. You can develop friendship as you love your mate with all of your heart (emotional part of life), soul (the spiritual), strength (the physical), and the mind (mental part of life). The joint activities and interest become enhanced because you have your special person to share them with. When you create a connection, you get more out of things you do together, for you are best friends. Having friendship in a marriage creates a place where you both can share your deepest thoughts and feelings. You feel accepted and get each other's approval, so you know that it's okay to open up and be vulnerable. This makes you more interesting to your spouse in a way that you want to know how they feel and what they think, and what makes them tick.

Love Each Other:

Husbands and wives should love each other unconditionally. How you love will cause a great impact on your marriage. Love will bring comfort to your marriage. Always strive to give your spouse your best love. Love in marriage is not just romance; it's a real and constant affection and care for each other with a passionate heart. Real love is never based on your wealth or your beauty, for these things will pass away. The most important thing that you should base your love on is God's word. True love in marriage covers a multitude of things. Having love in your marriage works patience. When you keep love alive, the marriage will flourish.

Being Patient:

Having patience in marriage is very important. Patience is having the ability to refrain yourself from reacting in anger, this causes less arguments and fights. In marriage, you have to work on having patience. It's not an overnight process, but the more both of you work on it, the more the two of you will develop patience. Patience will come with time. The Bible states, "Be completely humble and gentle; be patient, bearing with one another in love." (Ephesians 4:2).

Serve Each Other:

In a marriage, serving each other is so important. When you serve your spouse, it should be a privilege and an honor to do so. Serving each other should be done with joy, simply doing what needs to be done from your hearts. When doing it this way, it paves the way to let your spouse know how much you care. This will make your marriage healthy and happy. There are many ways to help serve one another, by taking turns cooking and washing the laundry, and the list goes on. My husband and I enjoy serving each other.

Look Out for Each Other's Interest in All Things:

Always have your partner's best interest. No matter what, you both should always have each other's backs. The husband and wife should be best friends, laughing and weeping together, with nothing but death separating their interest. In a marriage, you should enhance one another's good reputation. It means so much to know that your spouse is walking with you in agreement. God's word tells us in Amos 3:3 "Can two people walk together without agreeing on directions?"

Staying Faithful to Each Other:

Being faithful in marriage is so important; being able to trust each other causes your marriage to be healthy. God tells us in his word that every man should have sex with his own wife and every wife with her own husband (1 Corinthians 7:2). Faithfulness in a marriage is giving your spouse positive reasons to be faithful. It involves keeping each other's secret. Staying faithful keeps your marriage strong and healthy.

Pray for Each Other:

Praying for each other in marriage is very vital. Take time out to pray together as a family, because a family that prays together stays together. Praying for your marriage keeps your marriage from being attacked by the enemy because the adversary will rise up; prayer changes things. Make sure that you pray for God's peace in your home and in your marriage. Always be determined to speak positive words about your marriage. Prayer is the glue that holds a marriage and family together. Lift up each other in prayer. It works!

1 Corinthians 7:1-40

"Now concerning the matters about which you wrote: 'It is good for a man not to have sexual relations with a woman.' But because of the temptation to sexual immorality, each man should have his own wife and each woman her own husband. The husband should give to his wife her conjugal rights, and likewise the wife to her husband. For the wife does not have authority over her own body, but the husband does. Likewise the husband does not have authority over his own body, but the wife does. Do not deprive one another, except perhaps by agreement for a limited time, that you may devote yourselves to prayer; but then come together again, so that Satan may not tempt you because of your lack of self-control."

1 Corinthians 13:4-7

"Love is patient and kind; love does not envy or boast; it is not arrogant or rude. It does not insist on its own way; it is not irritable or resentful; it does not rejoice at wrongdoing, but rejoices with the truth. Love bears all things, believes all things, hopes all things, endures all things."

Ephesians 5:22-33

"Wives, submit to your own husbands, as to the Lord. For the husband is the head of the wife even as Christ is the head of the church, his body, and is himself its Savior. Now as the church submits to Christ, so also wives should submit in everything to their husbands. Husbands, love your wives, as Christ loved the church and gave himself up for her, that he might sanctify her, having cleansed her by the washing of water with the word . . ."

Genesis 2:24

"Therefore a man shall leave his father and his mother and hold fast to his wife, and they shall become one flesh."

Proverbs 18:22

"He who finds a wife finds a good thing and obtains favor from the Lord."

Hebrews 13:4

"Let marriage be held in honor among all, and let the marriage bed be undefiled, for God will judge the sexually immoral and adulterous."

Proverbs 21:9

"It is better to live in a corner of the housetop than in a house shared with a quarrelsome wife."

Proverbs 19:14

"House and wealth are inherited from fathers, but a prudent wife is from the Lord."

Matthew 19:2-9

"And large crowds followed him, and he healed them there. And Pharisees came up to him and tested him by asking, 'Is it lawful to divorce one's wife for any cause?' He answered, 'Have you not read that he who created them from the beginning made them male and female,' and said, 'Therefore a man shall leave his father and his mother and hold fast to his wife, and the two shall become one flesh'? So they are no longer two but one flesh. What therefore God has joined together, let not man separate."

1 Corinthians 7:39

"A wife is bound to her husband as long as he lives. But if her husband dies, she is free to be married to whom she wishes, only in the Lord."

Malachi 2:13-16

"And this second thing you do. You cover the Lord's altar with tears, with weeping and groaning because he no longer regards the offering or accepts it with favor from your hand. But you say, 'Why does he not?' Because the Lord was witness between you and the wife of your youth, to whom you have been faithless, though she is your companion and your wife by covenant. Did he not make them one, with a portion of the Spirit in their union? And what was the one God seeking? Godly offspring. So guard yourselves in your spirit, and let none of you be faithless to the wife of your youth. 'For the man who does not love his wife but divorces her,' says the Lord, 'the God of Israel, covers his garment with violence,' says the Lord of hosts. So guard yourselves in your spirit, and do not be faithless."

2 Corinthians 6:14

"Do not be unequally yoked with unbelievers. For what partnership has righteousness with lawlessness? Or what fellowship has light with darkness?"

Ephesians 5:31

"Therefore a man shall leave his father and mother and hold fast to his wife, and the two shall become one flesh."

Ephesians 5:25

"Husbands, love your wives, as Christ loved the church and gave himself up for her . . ."

Ephesians 5:33

"However, let each one of you love his wife as himself, and let the wife see that she respects her husband."

Matthew 5:32

"But I say to you that everyone who divorces his wife, except on the ground of sexual immorality, makes her commit adultery, and whoever marries a divorced woman commits adultery."

1 Corinthians 7:12-15

"To the rest I say (I, not the Lord) that if any brother has a wife who is an unbeliever, and she consents to live with him, he should not divorce her. If any woman has a husband who is an unbeliever, and he consents to live with her, she should not divorce him. For the unbelieving husband is made holy because of his wife, and the unbelieving wife is made holy because of her husband. Otherwise your children would be unclean, but as it is, they are holy. But if the unbelieving partner separates, let it be so. In such cases the brother or sister is not enslaved. God has called you to peace."

Psalm 85:10

"Steadfast love and faithfulness meet; righteousness and peace kiss each other."

1 Corinthians 11:11

"Nevertheless, in the Lord woman is not independent of man nor man of woman;"

1 Peter 3:1-11

"Likewise, wives, be subject to your own husbands, so that even if some do not obey the word, they may be won without a word by the conduct of their wives, when they see your respectful and pure conduct. Do not let your adorning be external—the braiding of hair and the putting on of gold jewelry, or the clothing you wear—but let your adorning be the hidden person of the heart with the imperishable beauty of a gentle and quiet spirit, which in God's sight is very precious. For this is how the holy women who hoped in God used to adorn themselves, by submitting to their own husbands . . ."

Matthew 19:9

"And I say to you: whoever divorces his wife, except for sexual immorality, and marries another, commits adultery."

Hosea 2:19

"And I will betroth you to me forever. I will betroth you to me in righteousness and in justice, in steadfast love and in mercy."

Hebrews 13:1-25

"Let brotherly love continue. Do not neglect to show hospitality to strangers, for thereby some have entertained angels unawares. Remember those who are in prison, as though in prison with them, and those who are mistreated, since you also are in the body. Let marriage be held in honor among all, and let the marriage bed be undefiled, for God will judge the sexually immoral and adulterous. Keep your life free from love of money, and be content with what you have, for he has said, 'I will never leave you nor forsake you.'"

1 Peter 3:1

"Likewise, wives, be subject to your own husbands, so that even if some do not obey the word, they may be won without a word by the conduct of their wives."

Isaiah 62:5

"For as a young man marries a young woman, so shall your sons marry you, and as the bridegroom rejoices over the bride, so shall your God rejoice over you."

1 Corinthians 11:12

"For as woman was made from man, so man is now born of woman. And all things are from God."

Proverbs 21:19

"It is better to live in a desert land than with a quarrelsome and fretful woman."

Mark 10:12

"And if she divorces her husband and marries another, she commits adultery."

1 Timothy 3:2

"Therefore an overseer must be above reproach, the husband of one wife, sober-minded, self-controlled, respectable, hospitable, able to teach . . ."

Jeremiah 29:6

"Take wives and have sons and daughters; take wives for your sons, and give your daughters in marriage, that they may bear sons and daughters; multiply there, and do not decrease."

Romans 7:1-3

"Or do you not know, brothers—for I am speaking to those who know the law—that the law is binding on a person only as long as he lives? For a married woman is bound by law to her husband while he lives, but if her husband dies she is released from the law of marriage. Accordingly, she will be called an adulteress if she lives with another man while her husband is alive. But if her husband dies, she is free from that law, and if she marries another man she is not an adulteress."

1 Corinthians 7:24-40

"So, brothers, in whatever condition each was called, there let him remain with God. Now concerning the betrothed, I have no command from the Lord, but I give my judgment as one who by the Lord's mercy is trustworthy. I think that in view of the present distress it is good for a person to remain as he is. Are you bound to a wife? Do not seek to be free. Are you free from a wife? Do not seek a wife. But if you do marry, you have not sinned, and if a betrothed woman marries, she has not sinned. Yet those who marry will have worldly troubles, and I would spare you that. . ."

1 Corinthians 13:1-13

"If I speak in the tongues of men and of angels, but have not love, I am a noisy gong or a clanging cymbal. And if I have prophetic powers, and understand all mysteries and all knowledge, and if I have all faith, so as to remove mountains, but have not love, I am nothing. If I give away all I have, and if I deliver up my body to be burned, but have not love, I gain nothing.

1 John 4:7

"Beloved, let us love one another, for love is from God, and whoever loves has been born of God and knows God."

Exodus 22:16

"If a man seduces a virgin who is not betrothed and lies with her, he shall give the bride-price for her and make her his wife."

Hosea 2:20

"I will betroth you to me in faithfulness. And you shall know the Lord."

1 Corinthians 7:1-6

"Now concerning the matters about which you wrote: "It is good for a man not to have sexual relations with a woman." But because of the temptation to sexual immorality, each man should have his own wife and each woman her own husband. The husband should give to his wife her conjugal rights, and likewise the wife to her husband. For the wife does not have authority over her own body, but the husband does. Likewise the husband does not have authority over his own body, but the wife does. Do not deprive one another, except perhaps by agreement for a limited time, that you may devote yourselves to prayer; but then come together again, so that Satan may not tempt you because of your lack of self-control. . ."

Genesis 2:22-25

"And the rib that the Lord God had taken from the man he made into a woman and brought her to the man. Then the man said, 'This at last is bone of my bones and flesh of my flesh; she shall be called Woman, because she was taken out of Man.' Therefore a man shall leave his father and his mother and hold fast to his wife, and they shall become one flesh. And the man and his wife were both naked and were not ashamed."

Ezekiel 16:8

"When I passed by you again and saw you, behold, you were at the age for love, and I spread the corner of my garment over you and covered your nakedness; I made my vow to you and entered into a covenant with you, declares the Lord God, and you became mine."

Romans 7:2

"For a married woman is bound by law to her husband while he lives, but if her husband dies she is released from the law of marriage."

Genesis 1:27

"So God created man in his own image, in the image of God he created him; male and female he created them."

Ephesians 3:14-21

"For this reason I bow my knees before the Father, from whom every family in heaven and on earth is named, that according to the riches of his glory he may grant you to be strengthened with power through his Spirit in your inner being, so that Christ may dwell in your hearts through faith—that you, being rooted and grounded in love, may have strength to comprehend with all the saints what is the breadth and length and height and depth . . .”

1 Corinthians 6:16

“Or do you not know that he who is joined to a prostitute becomes one body with her? For, as it is written, 'The two will become one flesh.'”

Luke 16:18

“Everyone who divorces his wife and marries another commits adultery, and he who marries a woman divorced from her husband commits adultery.”

Matthew 19:29

“And everyone who has left houses or brothers or sisters or father or mother or children or lands, for my name's sake, will receive a hundredfold and will inherit eternal life.”

In a marriage, you have to respect each other and demonstrate it. Find something that you both love to do together. Most of all, treasure each other. Marriage involves change, trust, and acceptance; it begins with love. My husband and I, after twenty-nine years of marriage, demonstrate our love for each other every day. We respect each other for the glory of God. The Lord is behind it all, and we try to overlook each other's faults. You must respect each other's differences because God made each one of us different. Keep priorities in perspective, agree and compromise on the big things, and don't create crisis over the small things. Share common interests and support each other's individual pursuits. View your time together as a gift and make it periodically special by breaking the routine.

In a marriage, conflicts will arrive. Try to understand the intents of the words, and not the speaker of the words, always be open to hear one another. Speak peace and life to your marriage! Proverbs tells us "The mouth of the righteous is a foundation of life." It's very important that you take time out to eat dinner together and share your thoughts, learn to relax and enjoy family fellowship communication and enjoy hearing from each other about what's going on in their lives. Time spent together is awesome, just listening at the dinner table is valuable and it allows the family to see how important eating together, there's nothing like spending quality time together. Praying together is much needed in families; a family that prays together stays together. Take time out of your busy schedule to enjoy your spouse. We understand that we live in a busy world, too busy to spend time together. Make sure to make time for each other and ensure that it's quality. Make your spouse a priority and set time for them first before making time for your goals and the things that interest you. Your marriage should be on the very top of your list.

Appreciate your spouse, it's so important to let your spouse know how much you appreciate them. Always let your spouse know how much you appreciate them for everything they do, by demonstrating gratitude in thoughtful ways. Telling your spouse thanks goes a long ways in a marriage--- it helps build confidence and takes your love for each other to another level. It is so important to acknowledge your partner, telling your spouse how grateful you are to have each other in your life; this helps you maintain a healthy marriage. Sometimes, showing your appreciation to your spouse can be easily forgotten, but it can really make a world of difference in their attitude toward you and their daily tasks. Just to say "I appreciate you" can make each other's day. Always highlight the things that they are good at and let them know exactly how much you appreciate who they are, and how special they are in your life.

Forgive your spouse, sometimes it's hard to ask for forgiveness but it's necessary to ask for forgiveness in a marriage. God tells us in his word that if we don't forgive each other, neither will he forgive us; it's so important to forgive your spouse. So many married couples make the greatest mistake of holding on to their hurts, rehashing them every time a new one comes along. Stop re-living your past hurt; forgive and move on. If you don't forgive and let go of your hurts, eventually it will build up and cause bitterness and resentment and ruin your marriage. Whatever you do, deal with your hurt and let them go once they've past. The moment you forgive the better off your marriage will be. Learn to forgive yourself and forgive your spouse; your marriage will be happy and healthy.

Recognize you are not perfect; face the truth that you are not the easiest person to live with. There're times when you are not always right, acknowledge that there has been times that you have made mistakes since you've been married. Think about it, be honest: you are not perfect! The sooner you realize that you are not perfect, you will not expect for your spouse to be perfect either. Focus on the positive things that you love about your partner and not the negative things that you dislike about your spouse and learn to pray for each other and work on your flaws together. God meant for you to be helpers one to another, and to help build each other up and not tear one another down. Strengthen each other.

In a marriage it's so important to invest your time and energy, a marriage is like anything else: whatever you put into it is what you get out of it. In a marriage, it requires a lot of energy and time; you only get what you deposit in. Time and energy are greatly needed for a great union. You have to spend precious hours, year after year, trying to get that great reward just as you work toward anything that you are trying to accomplish in life. There's no difference in a marriage: it takes hard work, dedication, commitment, your time and energy and love. The time that you invest in a marriage is for a lifetime and upkeep is necessary until death do you part. Investing time for one another in a marriage is extremely important.

Always apologize for anything you said or done to hurt your partner. When you apologize, do so sincerely from your heart. "I'm sorry" is one of the shortest yet most important sentences in a marriage; a heartfelt apology goes a long way. Show your partner how much you care about their feelings by telling them that you are sorry. Let them know that you are sorry if you have offended them in anyway. Listen to your spouse if they share with you that you hurt their feelings. After all, we all have feelings; have compassion and sympathy and apologize for anything you said, big are small. It shouldn't hurt you to say that you apologize for something you said wrong, are something you just did wrong. Always remember in a marriage that Communication is the key to a good and solid marriage!

Chapter 2

Priority

It's so crucial after a wedding to put Christ first. After you marry, it's vital that your relationship becomes top priority, even more than your children. Why? Because strong families are not built around children. They are built on strong marriages. In order for your marriage to be strong, you have to prioritize it, you have to work on it, pursue it. I am a strong, firm believer that this works! I'm not telling you to neglect your children because they are very important. But they are not as important as your marriage. Please don't neglect your marriage for the sake of your children; your marriage will suffer, it will cause conflicts and might even cause a divorce. When your marriage suffers, so do your children.

As a role model, you need to show your children a successful marriage. Raising kids is a temporary assignment in your life.

One day your children are going to leave home. They are going to grow up and have to leave your care, but your marriage is until death do you part. Spouses who neglect their marriages for their children are headed for a lot of aches and pains. Think about it, when the children leave the house, who will be left? You and your spouse. Those spouses only have a shell of a marriage left. Your children will not have a successful marriage to imitate when they get married. Not only will your marriage suffer, but your children will suffer also. Indeed, your children are important, precious, and priceless, but make sure you are prioritizing and balancing your care for them as well as your care for your marriage.

By setting an example and by giving your spouse the attention and love they deserve, you are teaching your children to love and respect their spouses when they marry, by working hard at your marriage. When we set great examples, we become our children's role model, and we prepare the way for them and their future. Building a foundation that extends far beyond the childbearing years gives our children hope to know that they can have a beautiful union too.

We are living in a busy world; it can be difficult to make time for one another. If you don't make time for your spouse and family, it will begin to fall apart. You will miss out on those important events and dates, and you will begin to lose the bond that you once had. Whatever you do, make time for your spouse and never take your marriage for granted. There are many married couples who make other areas of their life a priority and assume that their spouse will be there when they are finished with everything. It's meant to be the other way around. It doesn't work like that! Make sure your spouse is a priority and set time with them first, before making time for all your special events and goals, etc. Make sure when you make time that it's quality time.

Marriage should be our high priority. My husband and I prioritized our marriage with Christ being first, him being the head over our family. Why is prioritizing so important in marriage? Lack of priority can cause conflicts. If we don't put Christ first, our spouse second, otherwise you will have all kinds of problems and wonder why your marriage is so jacked up, why your children aren't following authority or following instructions, etc. If you put all your time on your children and all your needs, wants, and difficulties, they will start thinking that you are supposed to serve them all the times. After they grow up and leave home, they have the privilege and honor of having their own families.

Prioritizing your marriage is one of the most important things you can do every day. Priority is reflected on every day choices you give to your spouse. Prioritizing your marriage starts with putting Christ first; doing this will cause your union to flourish. Marriage should be your highest priority beside God being first. Making Christ head over your life, over your marriage, and above all outside activities and friends, parents, and in-laws. Why is prioritizing in marriage so vital? How do the lack of priority cause conflict in marriage? God created a woman for a man, and the man was created to be head over his wife (Genesis 2: 20:24). The husband is the head and the wife is the neck, a head without a neck is *no-good*! Husbands and wives are to function as teammates; however, God didn't ordain for it to be two heads in a household. Anything with two heads is a monster and needs to be killed.

God took the woman from the man's side intentionally, not from his head that he might rule over her, not from his feet that he should walk over her, but from the side as his helpmeet near his heart, and under his arm for protection. When we set your priority right with God being first, our spouse second; otherwise, we will run into all kinds of heartaches and problems. You may be wondering why isn't your marriage flourishing in the right order, or why your children are not respecting authority or following instructions. Anytime you don't prioritize in the way that God intended you to do, putting your children, friend's, activities, parents, eventually you will lose connection with your spouse. I can truly say when you do it God's way, this will cause your marriage and family unit to be filled with great joy.

God created Adam first, then he gave Adam a wife. The children came later, after they were out of the Garden of Eden. Then came Adam's life, a job, and much later, fellowship among believers. The fellowship among believers came after his other priorities. A priority is not measured by how much time we spend with others. Priorities are determined by their level of importance; more often than not, our children or job needs more time in comparison to our other priorities. If we follow this order of importance, then we may avoid making wrong decisions and have a big negative impact on the other priorities. If you believe that your church is of a higher priority over your spouse, then you are setting your marriage up for a great divorce! God and the church are two different levels: the church is not God, and God is not the church. They are two different and distinct priorities.

Always make God first in your life, you would go a long way keeping everything else in order. Luke 10:27 says, "And he answered, you should love the Lord your God with all of your heart and with all your soul and with all your strength with all your mind, and your neighbor as yourself." When you put God first, then everything else will fall in line. It takes commitment from you that you yield your will to God's will. God first then your spouse is next. God ordained a marriage before he ordained a ministry.

It is so sad to say that the divorce rate amongst Christians is no different than non-Christians. This shouldn't be. I believe that some divorces are caused by not putting God first, lack of communication, commitment, trust, prioritize, submission, finances problems, respect, love, and insecurity, etc.

There are other ways to prioritize your marriage as parents. You can show a lot of affection in front of your children, little hugs, telling each other how much you love one another, sitting close to each other, holding hands, playing and teasing each other, or giving one another a kiss. Show your children the same love you both have for them by given them hugs and kisses, have times to sit around, to laugh and tease and enjoy each other's conversations. It's good for them to see the love that you both share. We are role models for our children's future when they decide to get married.

Know your place in your marriage when it comes between both of you and your family. My husband and I learned to weigh very carefully what commitments we will make to others, activities that we will participate in, and what outside activities with friends! We enjoy going and there are the house of worship, the times when we study the word of God together. As a family we enjoy eating dinner and praying together.

Charity starts at home then it spreads aboard. Our greatest ministry is at home—you have to choose what works best for your family. Make sure you keep your marriage in the right perspective. My husband and I enjoy serving our family, then there comes a little "flex time" as well; our family health and unity is top priority. We also utilize our time and God-given talents to serve others.

Chapter 3

The Husband's Role

The first duty of the husband is to love his wife. The word *love* has become a misunderstood word. Love is an action word; most people have taken this word out of context. Love is an action word and it goes deep, it has been described the lust of the flesh, and nothing more. The Bible mentions the word love talking about sacrifice that you make for the betterment of someone else. You can measure love by your sacrifice, not by your enjoyment. To say that a man loves his wife is a talk about sacrifice that he makes for her (Ephesians 5:25). "Husbands, love your own wives, even as Christ loved the church, and gave himself for it." Husbands honor and love your wives; you should treat her like a queen. She's not just another woman, and love has to do with appreciating her, giving her special treatment.

Ask yourself a question, "Do your spouse feel special?" Many husbands do for other women what they wouldn't do for their own wives. That's a shame! This relates to some men—there was a time when you use to open the car door for your wife and hold the door when entering a public place; now she's opening the door for herself. She's your queen, you should make her feel very special. Do you make your wife feel special? By the good treatments you give her, by the actions you show her from your heart. I just wanted to call you, to tell you how much I love you, missing you, can't wait to see your beautiful face. These kind words will set off a spark. If she's away from home, she would try to beat you home! Every now and then buy her a gift. It doesn't have to be a dozen roses, one rose will do; and writing a note to let her know just how much you care will mean so much.

Too many men stop honoring their wives once they have been married for a long period of time. When was the last date? I'm not talking about the last time you came home and said, "What do you want to do tonight?" That's not a date. I'm talking about, "Hey I got a plan, all you have to do is come along for the ride." Even if it's just a ride out in the country.

Husbands, love your wife, don't be harsh with them," Colossians 3:19. "Husbands, in the same way be considerate as you live with your wives, and treat them with respect as the weaker partner with you of the gracious gift of life, so that nothing will hinder your prayers (1 Peter 3:7). Men, it's important to treat your wife with respect and love. The Lord desires that the man cares for and love his wife. God did not create woman, for the man to Lord over her. God created man and woman both to compliment to each other through a healthy companionship. The Bible speaks of the role of a husband to fulfill companionship through the heart.

Husbands love your wives, just as Christ loved the church and gave himself up for her to make her holy, cleansing her by the washing with water through the word, and to present her to himself as a radiant church, without stain or wrinkle or any blemish, but holy and blameless. Husbands, you ought to love your wives as you love yourself. A man that loves his wife loves himself. The relationship between a husband and a wife is meant to be one of love, respect, and support. God intended for the husband to care for his spouse and provide for his family.

The Word of God states that a man who doesn't take care of his household is worse than an unbeliever. God expects you to take good care of your bride and your household. After all, a wife is a beautiful, special gift given to you from God. When someone dear to you presents a gift to you, what do you do with it? Do you cherish it? Well, that's the same way God expects you to do with your wife: love and to cherish every moment of that special gift that he has presented to you.

In the very beginning of time when God created Adam, he said that man needed a helpmeet, a suitable helper. He stated in his word that it wasn't good for man to be alone. Genesis 2-20:24 says "But for Adam no suitable helper was found. So the Lord God caused the man to fall into a deep sleep and while he was sleeping, he took one of the man's ribs and then closed up the place with flesh. Then the Lord God made a woman from the rib he had taken out of man. God created man and woman with natural, physical, and emotional differences usually where one is weak, the other is strong. Therefore God created the two to help meet each other's needs.

Husbands, love is an action word. Apostle John wrote in one of his letters, let us not love with words or tongues, but with actions and in truth (1 John 3:18). Most times in the homes, sacrificial action is missing. Ask yourself when was the last time you gave up something of value for your wife, like a fishing trip or your favorite game on TV. Sometimes, you need to give up something so that you can spend some quality time with your wife so that she can see your love. Serving your wife and being the head of your house don't mean that you are to lord over her life. Christ is our example for this type of leadership. Jesus didn't just talk about being a servant; he also demonstrated being a servant when he washed the feet of his disciples. Jesus didn't come to be served but he came to serve (John 3 1:17). Christ the head of the church took on the very nature of a servant when he was made in human likeness (Philippians 2:7). Husbands, one of the best ways to serve your wife is to understand what her needs are. Men, serving your wives means providing for her. This provision involve assuming the responsibility for meeting her material needs. 1 Timothy 5:8 states, "But if anyone does not provide for his own, especially for those of his household, he denied the faith, and is worse than an unbeliever." A servant is to accommodate the gift of your life that God has given you. You are to be a leader, a lover, a provider.

Husbands, if you love and serve your wife in the way God commanded you to do, at the judgment seat of Christ you will hear him say "Well done thou good and faithful servant." Your love for your wife should be unconditional. This love for her shouldn't be based on the things that she does for you but her worth as God's great gift to you. Verbally let her know how much you love and value her.

The marital responsibility of husbands Is to love your wives, The Greek Word rendered "love" is agapso, which denotes the willing sacrificial giving on the husband's part for the benefit of his wife, without thought of return. As Christ gave himself for the church, so there is to be no sacrifice, not even the laying down of his life, that a husband should not be willing to make for his wife. As the church is part of Jesus' body, so is the wife a part of her husband's body. Thus, when the husband loves her, he loves himself. As a man who cares for his body benefits himself, so a husband so the husband who loves his wife brings much profit to himself.

Christ simply instructed the husband to love his wife just as Christ loved the church; this is every husband's duty. The Lord intended for the man to love, respect, and care for his wife. Even though a woman is capable of taking care of herself, God made men and women different and this is due to the physical nature and strength God has given man. He has charged them to provide and protect his family. This physical strength that God gave man is to be managed with grace and gentleness.

The Lord didn't create man to lord over his wife nor did he make woman to wait on man. He made them both to be helpers one to another. The relationship between a husband and wife is meant to be one of love, respect, and support. Both are helpers to each other! This plan is talked about in the book of Genesis.

God saw that it wasn't good for man to be alone so he made a suitable helpmeet so he created Eve. Genesis 2:20-24 says, "But for Adam No suitable helper was found so the Lord God caused the man to fall into a deep sleep; and while he was sleeping he took one of the man's ribs and closed up the place with flesh. Then the Lord God made a women from the rib he had taken out of the man, and he brought her to man. The man said, 'This is now bone of my bones and flesh of my flesh; she shall be called "woman," for she was taken out of man.' That is why a man leaves his father and mother and is united to his wife, and they become one flesh."

This also leads to another understanding of companionship. God created man and woman with natural, physical, and emotional differences. Most times where one is weak, the other is strong.

Therefore, a husband and wife can help each other out by meeting each other's needs through physical and emotional intimacy. 1 Corinthians 7:2-5 states, "But since sexual immorality is occurring, each man should have sexual relations with his own wife, and each woman with her own husband.

The husband should fulfill his marital duty to his wife, and likewise the wife to her husband. The wife do not have authority over her own body but yields it to her husband. In the same way, the husband does not have authority over his own body but yields it to his wife. Do not deprive each other except perhaps by mutual consent and for a time, so that you may devote yourselves in prayer. Then come together again Satan will not tempt you because of lack of self-control." When the needs of your spouse are properly met through a healthy relationship, the two can help each other and can live a successful life together. Roles of the husband in the Bible is so crucial being fulfilled by a strong man of God, because Satan desires to destroy the family unit, but through Christ and the proper knowledge of the word of God about biblical roles, the family will be strong in the Lord.

One of the main roles of a husband in the Bible is to be a leader of his wife and family. Leadership plainly means to guide and influence his family. Therefore a Christian husband should be a great example and teach his family the way of the Lord. The Lord doesn't give a husband power to rule over his wife; instead he should impact his wife and family with the word of God.

Husbands should demonstrate with their voice and their effort, behavior, and characteristics that bring glory to God and value to their spouse and family.

When the husband produces good spiritual fruits based on the Bible he becomes strong, and confident that he's leading his family in the way of the Lord. Husbands, you are the thermostat, you control the temperature. Your wife is the thermometer; she'll let you know exactly what it reads. Most time a wife knows exactly what's going on with her husband; she can tell by the look on his face because she is his mirror. Husbands, make it a habit to pray with your wife and your family.

Always pray together as a family because a family that prays together stays together. If there's no spiritual relationship in the home, there won't be a great relationship in the marriage. Once you are married, it's no more singular relationship with God because the both of you have become "one flesh." God will not treat you apart from her, simple fact he doesn't see two people any more. He sees you as one flesh. Ephesians 5:25 says "Husbands love your wives, just as Christ also loved the church and gave himself for her, to make her holy, cleansing her in the washing of water by the power of his word." He did this to present the church to himself in splendor, without spot or wrinkle or any such things but holy and blameless.

In the same way, husbands should love their wives as their own bodies. He who loves his wife loves himself. For no one ever hates his own flesh, but provides and cares for it, just as Christ does for the church, since we are members of his body. For this reason, a man will leave his father and mother and be joined to his wife, and the two will become one flesh. This is deep from the heart, talking about the church as well as Christ. Husbands, cherish every moment with your wife. You've been joined together by God, don't let nothing or anything come between the love that you have for your wife. Love her unconditionally, let her know that she is far above rubies; praise her when she does well.

Chapter 4

The Wife's Role

One of my great roles as a wife, mother and grandmother is a joy serving my family. This is a great part of my life. I truly enjoy being married these twenty nine blessed years of my life. The Lord has kept us together a total of thirty five years and we are still in love. Marriage is a great role to play. Being a woman married with nine children I understand what God's will is for me, to be the wife and mother he intended and ordained me to be. Being the wife that God called me to be, my first priority is to take care of my family, to train up my children in the way of the Lord and to build my husband into the man he's called to be. Those three things or no easy job and often looked over in the world as a throwback or as something the women in today's world don't focus on much. I truly believe families would be much stronger if women will stand up and take back their femininity and invest more time and more of their strength and power in their families. (Joshua 24:15) says, As for me and my house we will serve the Lord. Dare to say it's almost easier to climb the corporate ladder?

We as women all have different situations in life that dictate the way we live. It's a test to see beyond the family beyond the glory beyond the next self-fulfilling goal and focus on being the, greatest wife the greatest mom and the greatest caretaker in my home that my family could ever have. I am no exceptions to any of that. Being a woman and playing the role of a wife is a powerful role that God has given each one of us. I love the way in which God helps us to focus on those priorities and live out our desires to be the good wife that he has called us to be. I get great joy being a helpmeet. The Lord has intended for the two of us to become one. I can truly say that in my house hold that my husband is the head and I'm the neck to help support. For me that equals comfort, and strength that I don't have to try to have on my own. Believe me I'm not a pushover or a door mat. I love being a feminine woman who voice is heard; I also love that my husband has the final say so. When marriages operate as God outlines it in the Scriptures, where man and woman are given different roles in a marriage, I believe that the family will flow like a Well-Oil Machine!

A wife is a woman joined in a marriage to a man, a woman considered in relation to her husband. The first duty of a woman is to her husband, is to submit to her husband, help him in and out of the house. This should be one of the first things a woman should do to help her husband around the house, Proverbs 31-13:4, gathering wool and flax, she makes it service with her hands. She is like a ship training from a distant, so she processes her livelihood. Ephesian 5: 22-31, wives submit yourselves unto your husband as unto the Lord. For the husband is the head of the wife, even as Christ is the head of the church, and he is the savior of the body.

Therefore as the church is subject to Christ, so let the wives, be to their own husbands in everything. Love your husband, with affection; this affection is something that can be taught (learned) if needed. The wife should remember that upon her, to the greatest extent the duty of making her home a happy home. She should do nothing to make her husband feel uncomfortable either mentally are physically but on the other hand she should strive to do most of her ability to do whatever is best calculated to please him.

Everything a wife duty is, to fear, reverence and respect her husband both for his person and his position. This necessarily includes love because if she loves him, she will try to please him and avoid offending him. Loving, forgiven, and submitting do not mean that you become a doormat or indefinitely tolerate significantly destructive behavior.

Women today need a clear understanding of how they should relate to their husband. In fact, the significant social changes brought about by the women's movement over the last few decades have led to such confusion that the very idea of "roles" is repugnant to some. They feel as if someone have lost their identity and their freedom if they adhere to some type of "outdated standard. It's important for us to look clearly at what the Bible says on this subject. And while the Bible doesn't apply modern word "role" to marriage, the Scriptures are clear about the unique responsibilities God assigns to a wife. Be a helper to your husband. While all of us are called to help pursue others, the Bible places a special emphasis on this responsibility for wives. Genesis tells us that God realized it wasn't good for man to be alone, and he decided to make a helper suitable for him" (Genesis 2:18). It is interesting to note that the Hebrew meaning of the word helper in this passage is found hereafter in the Bible to refer only to God as he helps us. The fact that this same word is applied to a wife signifies that we women have been given tremendous power for good in our husband's to become all that God intended for them to be.

Respect your husband. In Ephesians 5:33, Paul says, the wife must respect her husband. "When you respect your command to love your husbands. Therefore, we must look at love from their perspective, not just our own. Surveys show that sex is one of a man's most important needs – if not the most important. When a woman resists intimacy, is uninterested, or it's only passively interested, her husband may fear rejection. It will cut at his self-image, tear him to the very center of his being, and create isolation. Your husband's sexual needs should be more important and higher on your priority list than housework, project activities, and children. It does not mean that you should think about sex all day and every day but it does mean that you find ways to remember your husband and his needs. It means that you save some of your energy for him. It keeps you from being selfish and living only for your own needs and wants. Maintaining the focus helps you defeat isolation in your marriage

As a wife you have Great responsibilities, to commit to your husbands. The word of God clearly states exactly what he expect in a marriage relationship. There are several verses in Ephesians 5:22 that says wives submit yourselves to your own husband, as unto the Lord, therefore, as a church is subject unto Christ, so that the wives be to their own husbands in everything. Nevertheless, let every one of you in particular so love his wife even as himself and the wife see that she reverence her husband. Then in 1 Peter 3:1 Likewise, the wives, be in subjection to your own husbands. None of these verses teaches that a woman are weaker, but her feminine mind, qualities preclude her being as well-endowed for leadership. This subjections does not mean the state of being completely submissive to and to be controlled by someone more powerful. It's all about the wife recognizing the leadership of her husband. The husband should be as loving to his wife as Christ loved the church.

A wife is to be loved like Christ loved the church as stated in Ephesians 5:25, she is to be honored as none other in 1 Peter 3:7, she is to be praised by her family. Proverbs 31:28. Here's a list of responsibility, to be sober, to love their husband to love their children to be discreet, chaste, keepers at home, good obedience to their own husbands, that the word of God be not blasphemed. Wives "To love their husbands" is a command. Too many times man believe it is only a sexual relationship and in the mind of some women, that is all they think they are good for. To love your husband means that the both of you are partners working together to achieve a goal. You can be thankful of his actions, efforts and work in supporting the family. You will do everything in your power to make him comfortable, and happy. As wives, God has given us a commanded and great Responsibility and Duties!!

Ladies be Submissive to your own husbands as the word of God states in (Ephesians 5-22:23). Wives submit to your own husband's as you do to the Lord, for the husband is the head of the house of the wife as Christ is the head of the church. The word of God does not mean for a woman to be a slave in bondage to that man, it's to be mutual submission and love. Submissions means to yield or to set yourself under: From this definition we see to yield to one another instead of demanding, our own way. Your husband is to be head of his household; he's to love his wife. When a woman submits unto her own husband she is actually submitting unto God.

A woman therefore does not submit because her husband deserves it, because she knows that it's pleasing to the Lord. There will be times in your marriage where your husband don't deserves or he's not worthy in a human perspective, but because of divine right, because God set the man over his wife she needs to yield. God sees everything and every man will be held accountable for his actions and wrong doings.

The role of a wife clearly states in the Bible that God made man and woman equal in relationship to Christ, the word give specific roles for both the husband and the wife in a marriage. **Ephesians 2:22-24** says "Wives submit to your husbands as the Lord. For the husband is the head of the wife, as Christ is the head of the body, his body of which the savior now as the church submits to their husbands in everything. Wives the role that we have to play is to help up lift and support our husbands. In the word of God there are certain priorities that describe Christ as being first, the husband, the wife and then the children. There are certain orders that we must follow, because that's how it works. We don't go for a doctor's visit and expect to be treated by the receptionist; we expect to be treated by the doctor, that's called order, we must have order in our marriages, this is how God designed it in his Blue Print for the family unit. God didn't design for the woman to be the head; he gave man charge over the wife. Wives you need to be obedient to your own husband, this doesn't mean that you don't have any thoughts of your own. Husbands and wives need to work together so that you are not constantly pulling in an opposite direction. This obedience doesn't mean that you are your husband's slave or maid servant, but rather you are sharing a common goal.

Wives you need to make sure that you be good keepers at home" this is a command that indicates a divided responsibility. When God created a woman, she was taken from the rib of man. A woman were not taken from his foot that we might be crushed underneath his feet. Neither were we taken from his head so we might rule over the man. We were taken from the rib of man so that we can be by his side continually. Husbands and wives are part of each other.

A worthy woman is described in the book of **Proverb 31:10-29.** A truly good wife is the most precious treasure a man can find! Her husband depends on her, and she never lets him down. She is good to him every day of her life, and with her own hands she gladly makes cloths. She is like a sailing ship that brings food from across the sea. She gets up before daylight to prepare food for her family and for her servants. She knows how to buy land and how to plant vineyard, and she always works hard. She knows when to buy or sell, and she stays busy until late at night. She spins her own cloths and she helps the poor and the needed. She fulfills her responsibilities with grace and strength. She's a blessing to her husband and family. Her family has warm clothing so she do not worry when it snows. She does her own sewing and everything she wears is beautiful. Her husband is well known and a respected leader in city. She make clothes to sell to the shop owners she takes good care of her family and is never lazy. Her children praise her, and with great pride her husband says, there are many good woman but you are the best. **Colossians 3: 18:** "Wives submit to your husbands, as it is fitting in the Lord. The role that the wife has to play is to encourage, and help her husband. When we try to make it anymore during any less, that's when we run into trouble. Being a wife or these twenty nine years and studying the word of God, I learned to respect my husband because he is the head of the house, and I'm the neck to help support my Boaz, and to fulfill my duties as a wife.

1Timothy 2:11 says, Let a woman learn quietly with all submissiveness. The Bible states that a wise woman builds her house. Women don't be as the foolish woman that build her house and tear it down with her own hands, but instead be like the wise woman who builds her house for the Glory of God. **Wives Work Your Duties!**

Wives you need to be patient and have some understanding with your husband and encourage and help your spouse through periods of crisis that he could not have weathered alone. A wise woman knows what it takes to build up her husband when he's down. Proverbs 14:1 tells us that a wise woman builds her house but a foolish woman tears her own house down with her own hands. A foolish women is one that's always on the phone gossiping, watching as the world turn, wont cook, don't keep a clean house, always meddling in other folks business. She's too busy doing everything but playing her role. Sad to say, that there's some foolish women that has destroyed their own homes with their own hands. Some foolish women that has exchanged their Boaz for Bo Bo. The different between Boaz and Bo Bo, Boaz is a Godly man verses Bo Bo being an ungodly man. A wise woman guards her mind from obsessive thoughts, by trusting in God and his sovereign control at all times over all circumstances. So I encourage you to be wise and take your role as a wife serious, it's vital that you play your role to glorify the Lord.

Wives, I believe that prayer is so **important in order to** have a successful marriage, because you are in inviting the spirit of Christ in, to have his way as he desires. We can't shape or fix our marriages, it's up to Christ because he knows what's best for us. I believe by praying for your husband can bring nothing but good, praying works for every aspect of his life. Wives you need to be prayer warriors for your husband and family. My heart desire is that my husband feel covered in prayer. Here are some Scriptures that you can Decree and Declare over your husband lives.

* That he would lean and depend on Christ when facing trials. **(Psalms 46:1).**
* That he would live according to God's Word. **(Ephesians 4:1-2).**
* That he would have a heart to give. **(Proverbs 28:27).**
* That he would trust God's plan for his life. **(Jeremiah 29:10).**
* That he would allow the Lord to be Lord over our marriage. **(Ephesians 5:29)**
* That he would give everything to the Lord in prayer. **(1 Thessalonians 5:17).**

* That the Lord would teach him to be the husband that he's called him to be. **(Ephesians 5:22-23).**
* That he will not live in fear but fear God. **(Psalms 118:6).**
* That he would grasp and understand God's purpose in Christ. **(Romans 8:28).**
* That he would boldly proclaim the gospel truth. **(Acts 28:31).**
* That he would be full of Peace and Patients. **(Romans 14:19).**
* That he would grow spiritually. **(2 Peter 3:18).**
* That he will be quick to forgive. **(1 Corinthians 13).**
* That he would humble himself and be teachable to the Holy Spirit. **(Proverbs 15:33).**

Sometimes it can be easy for us to allow bitterness towards our husband to set in our hearts, rather than thanking God for what he does you know exactly how the story goes, either he's working too late, the trash needs taken out are the clothes are not folded the way we want it to be are he don't say that he love you enough and the list goes on, most times this causes resentment to set into your hearts. Tell me that I'm not the only one that has experienced this? Oh good, you understand where I'm coming from. We as wives really can get right down angry and upset with our spouses, some of you get unappreciative and right down upset of his every move. Some even bark out orders as if to say that he's only there to serve your every needs.

Proverbs 14:1

Ladies; I'm a firm believer of what you give is what you get in return, as far as human behavior is concerned.

A good wife knows how to treat her husband; she knows how to love him. He will cherish you even the more, love you and nurture you in return. I'm a witness if you want to be treated like a queen then you need to treat him like a king!

Communication

Lack of communication in a marriage can cause conflicts. Communication is the key to a good and solid marriage. Always be opened, don't hid things from your husband or keep secrets after marriage. Be honest with your spouse find time to sit and commune with each other now if you don't take time out to communicate with your spouse, somebody else will step up to the plate and talk. Anytime you don't take the time out and share things with your husband and hold it in, this can and will cause trouble in your marriage, listen when your spouse is talking, learn how to be quiet and allow your spouse to speak and be a good listener when he speaks. You may have a lot of important things to talk about with your spouse, but allow him to talk first. The moment he comes home from work, please don't greet him with all of your problems and complaints, greet him with a kiss and a hug. Good communication helps build trust and strengthens your marriage. Don't take on any major decision without sharing them with your husband; talk it over with him this will keep down confusion and conflicts. Whenever you have problems or disagreements don't share them with the world, take time out to work it out, take your problems to the Lord in prayer.

Respect

Ladies build up your husbands; give him respect. If you are expecting respect from your husband you got to give some respect. Respect reflects in the way one talks and behaves, so be careful how you treat your spouse. Always speak in a loving way and refrain from speaking harshly. A good wife knows her place in her home; she gives her man respect and never chooses to put him down or embarrass or mistreat him in public. Watch what you say before speaking. Once a word is spoken, you can't take it back. A good wife speaks life and blessings to her hubby. She treats her husband with respect in front of others or at home. There's an old saying, "It's not so much of what you say but it's how you say it." Whatever you say, be sure to show respect to your husband.

Express Your Love and Appreciation

Ladies, your husbands like to be appreciated and yes he loves praises. They like to hear the word, "I love you." Show him how much you appreciate him, by cooking a good home-cooked meal or baking him his favorite dessert. Participate in some of his activities that he's interested in, even though you would like to be doing something else. Be there for him. Every once in a while, give him a gift; it's the little things that you do this counts. Pamper him by giving him a massage, run his bath water, or surprising him with his favorite dish. Allow him to miss you that gives him time to miss and to think about you. These gestures won't go unnoticed; this will cause him to do something nice. Don't withhold your feelings from your spouse; tell him how much you appreciate him for all that he does for you. Even the little things that he has done for you, tell him thanks and let him know how much you appreciate what he's done.

Be Supportive

Wives, your husbands need your support and understanding during times of trouble. One thing about a good wife, she will support her husband through his success and failures, she will comfort him, be there for him when he's feeling down and out. Wisely supporting your spouse goes a long way in marriage. Support your husband in all the positive things he does even in his career and life. Don't put your man down, build him up. A wife can make her husband or she can break him, keep him lifted up in prayer, encourage him with encouraging words, don't ever belittle your man. Don't criticize or embarrass your spouse in front of others, instead build him up. If you disagree with him, respectfully let him know in a kind way when you disagree with him.

Please Don't Nag

The worst thing that a man hates is a nagging wife. If you need him to do something, ask him in a nice way. There are so many wives that think by nagging her husband is the only way she can get him to move or do things. The truth is nagging can create a lot of problems and make matters worse between the both of you. Remember that your husband is a grown man with his own thoughts, all due respect, just because you need your husband to do something in particular that you want him to do, doesn't mean he has to do it. Trust me ladies nagging your husbands doesn't always work; most times this makes it worse, often it will cause the opposite of its intended affect. A man can't stand a nagging complaining wife, trust me if you need him to do something ask him in a kind way.

Keep Your Husband Happy in the Bedroom

Sexual intimacy is one of the most important things in a marriage, it's like a fresh breath of oxygen it helps take your marriage to another level, and Intimacy is not always physically. Just Some Good Old Fashion Romance. Wives when you please your man, he will accommodate you in many ways. Wives don't deprive yourself from your man even if you don't feel up to it. God tells us in, 1 Corinthians 7-5, "Deprive ye not for one another except it be with consent for a time, ye may give yourselves to fasting and prayer; and come together again, that Satan tempt you not for your incontinency" Ladies be pleasing to your husbands keep your spouse happy in bed.

Be Pleasant

Be kind to your husbands, it is said to treat others in the way that you want to be treated. Don't be rude to your man, be kind and polite, and treat him the way that you want be treated. Be polite when he ask you to do something, work toward being warm, positive and understanding to your hubby. When he comes home from work, welcome him with a kiss, hug and a smile instead of frown. A good wife knows how to be pleasing to her husband, yes she knows how to honor her king by keeping a pleasant tone in her voice, a happy smile on her face, and she keeps herself together looking good for her King when he arrives home. Always make him feel warm and welcome, especially after a hard day's of work. If you're not happy the way that your spouse is treating you, then take a minute and ask yourself a question as to how do you treat your partner, and correct your behavior.

Prepare the House

Ladies, whatever you do keep a clean house at all times, because a man love a clean place to call home, make him comfortable, after all his home should be his castle, he wants to be able to come home after a long hard days of work to a clean house and a good cooked meal, yes, even if you've worked, that's no excuse!

SANDRA WILSON

As a wife I enjoy playing my role. I don't take being married for granted. If it had not been for the Lord, on May 3, 2014, a night that will never be forgotten. Wilson racing was at the starting line at US 19 drag way. It was father against son, Larry Sr. vs. Larry Jr. On this particular night, just about the entire family was there. In the blink of the eye, chaos happened, a terrible accident at the end of the track not knowing whether it was my husband or my son. It was my husband that lost control of his car, flipping it over about ten times or more. This was the most frightening moment of my life. It was a long night in the emergency room with family and friends, waiting on the results of his condition. Thank God that he only suffered neck injuries, concussion, bruised lungs, and six palsy in his left eye that caused him to have double vision. He was admitted in the hospital for six days. Two days after being released from the hospital, on May 12, 2014, which was Mother's Day, another terrifying moment, after a long day with company and family, he became exhausted, and wanted to take a bath. After assisting him, he felt that he was able to give himself a bath. After leaving him to have some privacy, I went back into the dining room with my family. We were enjoying the company of each other. After my husband got out of the tub, I could hear that something was going wrong. At that moment, immediately my oldest son and I ran to the door. I asked him if he was okay, he replied yes. The moment he said yes, we heard him <u>collapsed</u> onto the floor, my son went in to assist his father. Shouts, screams, tears, and fear filled the house. Immediately my son called for his wife, who is a registered nurse, to come and help him. God is so good, an hour before my husband's incident, my son and his wife were about to leave, but the Lord had predestined them to stay.

(From Kortney) I arrived in the bathroom to the sight of my pop on the floor. His breathing was labored and his eyes were fixed open. I knelt down to talk to him and I noticed that he had taken his last breath. I waited a couple seconds for him to take another breath but he did not at that moment. I felt for a pulse and it was absent. At this moment I knew that I would have to perform CPR. I did not know how it was going to go. I am a nurse, and I have done CPR on many people in the hospital setting, but never alone and never on a loved one. I called my husband and told him that I needed him just to stay with me and help me through this. He came and stood by my side looking at me hovering over his father's lifeless body. Surprisingly, I felt a sense of peace at this time, I never panicked. My husband did not panic either. We were strong together and by him just being there with me gave me more strength to perform what needed to happen. I started CPR; I blew a series of breaths followed by chest compressions. It lasted for only about one cycle and when I rechecked his pulse he had a pulse. The pulse was pounding. I told my husband to feel his heartbeat through his chest. He then felt it; however, his breathing was extremely labored. He was still struggling to breathe. At this point, my husband and I started to pray asking God to touch and heal my father-in-law. We prayed and prayed and prayed without ceasing and his breathing started to get better. We asked him to wiggle his toes and he responded. We asked him his name, address, and he responded. We kept praying, touching, and agreeing that Pop was healed in the name of Jesus and he began to come back around. I witnessed a miracle on the bathroom floor at 1900. I am so honored that God saw fit to use me as a part of this great testimony. I learned so many lessons based on this experience and I am so grateful. This is something that I will *never* forget. I am so much stronger now. We don't always know God's plan, but it is my prayer that whatever he uses me to do that I'll do it for his glory.

Thanks to my daughter-in-law, my hero Kortney, and most of all for the *resurrecting power* of the Holy Spirit showing up and out, breathing life back into my husband.

I truly thank God for allowing my beloved husband another chance to still be here with me and my family. After his accident, he was out of work for several months. I can say that I was so honored to care for my husband and to nurse him back to good health, with the help of the Lord. I enjoy and cherish every moment with my husband. My love for my husband is indescribable. Ladies, I encourage you to enjoy and cherish every moment with your spouse because you don't even know what can happen in a blink of a moment. Wives, be submissive to your husbands and love him unconditionally. I understand if your spouse don't treat you the way that he should at times, still do your part as a wife and play your role for the glory of God.

Marriage is truly a beautiful gift that God has ordained. My husband and I are still deeply in love. I can truly say that happiness in marriage, and particularly in the role of a wife, is a very achievable goal. All it takes is willingness to see straight in the things that much of society calls weak, devotion, kindness, sympathy, femininity, and our true desire to turn to God above all things, even if needs be our spouse. Serenity will abound in the woman who knows who she is and where to turn for peace, and through that serenity she will have the power to help create the fairy tale relationship that many women dream about. I believe that I was created to be my husband's helpmeet, and that he is the principal figure in our home. I truly accept the role and honor it as a divine appointment from God. Wives, submit yourself to your own husbands as you do to the Lord.

Chapter 5

Keep the Fire Burning

Whether it's been several years or even several months, do you remember the vows that you made on your special day? You stood boldly before God, looking directly into those lovely eyes of your spouse and exchanged those awesome words. After that awesome vow was spoken, flames started flying high between the both of you, of unity and love. The joy poured out from the two of you. After being married after a long period of time, the fire may begin to go out; you have to do something to re-ignite the fire.

The key to keeping the fire burning in your marriage, you need to poke around in it to keep the fire burning. Don't let the flame Go Out! Sometimes in life you have to forget the small stuff and focus on the important things in life. Try to recapture the fire that you once had before you both became one and said "I Do." Take time out of your busy schedule, set aside a date with your spouse, go to dinner, out to a movie, or just to the park for a walk. Think back at the times when you first met and went out for dinner and how you both sat at the table with your arm around him/her. You talked and laughed, enjoyed the company, conducted yourselves like two lovebirds before the public.

The most important thing is not to focus on all of your activities but focus on enjoying each other. Reflect on the joyful experience you shared on your wedding day. Remember when you were dating, you didn't allow anything to come between you to cause you to cancel out your date. Whatever you do make sure that you spoil each other as often as you can!

Make it a habit to spoil each other. It's the little things that you do to keep your marriage alive, during lunchtime call your spouse, and if possible meet each other for lunch. It's the little act of thoughtfulness, you can score lots of points with your spouse, especially when they show them love and how much they care. God tells us in Romans 12:10, "Love one another with mutual affection; outdo one another in showing affection and honor and respect." Gaze upon your spouse, look them in the eyes and tell them how sexy they are and how good they look, put on your favorite lingerie and walk around in your bedroom and celebrate. Keep the fire burning, don't let your fire go out, sometimes you have to lay an extra log on the fire and keep it blazing. Placing one log on the fire daily so the flame will remain and grow.

Make sure you find a moment to hug and kiss your spouse before departing from one another. Trust me, this works; it adds energy to your relationship and makes life easier for each other's day. Seal each day with a good-bye kiss. The Song Of Solomon 1:2 "Let him/her kiss me with the kisses of his/her mouth! For your love is better than wine." Focus on what is right and not who! In a marriage, communication can become a daily challenge. Learn to speak with clarity and honesty. It's always good to think about your actions before you speak. Whenever your spouse talks, give him/her your undivided attention and listen to what he/she has to say.

A common issue in most marriages is usually after many years most times it can become a loss of spark. The work that goes into a successful marriage is constant and up keep is necessary. It takes a lot of energy and time, love, investment, dedication, communication, respect, commitment, submitting etc. but it is worth it, if you want your marriage to be successful, happy and long-lasting.

Think back when you first met the love of your life, it was like Fireworks! Both of you were excited and happy to be together. But as the years passed, reality set in and you found yourself waking up to the same person. Keep the passion in your relationship alive long after the fire. Just because you've been married ten, twenty, thirty, forty years don't mean that it's time to let the fire stop burning. My husband and I, after thirty-five years, have not allowed our fire to go out—it's still blazing greater now than ever before. Believe me, age does not play a factor; it's the love that you both have for each other.

Think about the things that makes your spouse great, think about the times when you first met and fell deeply in love and wanted to see each other every moment you got. Whatever it takes to rekindle your fire, do it! Whatever you do, enjoy your partner in spite of what comes your way. See what you can do to make his/her life better, work together to make each other happy, and keep the fire in your marriage enjoyable. Stroke the fire with some good old fashion Romance, play some good old love songs every now, and then purchase a gift. Don't let it become a birthday or valentine routine.

Take time to commune together. Communication is the key to a healthy and successful relationship. Concentrate on what you are talking about; it's about looking each other in the eyes and really discuss things. Whatever you do, don't let your "intimate moments" get *boring*. Enjoy each other in your own special room; relationships would be incomplete without intimate conversations. Go out on a date, book a romantic dinner for two. Don't get stuck in the same old routine, doing the same old thing; this become stalled and boring. Keep the fire burning. Take a trip for the weekend, do something different go someplace where you have never been before just for the sake of it and break the routine.

Keep the spark alive! Don't stop loving each other, it takes work in keeping the fire burning and it takes the both of you to keep the relationship alive. Always tell your spouse "I Love You." Never take for granted that your spouse knows that you love them; make sure that you tell them verbally! There's not a day that goes by that my husband and I tell each other how much we love one another! Keep the fire burning!! Stay on your honeymoon!

There are many things that married couples can do to help strengthen their marriage and divorce-proof their relationship. Keep the fire burning in your marriage!

Remember the time when you first met you always looked your best, smelled your best for the love of your life, keep it up. Always look your best for your spouse; husbands look good for your sweetheart, wives look good for your darling. Dress to impress your spouse! Wear your best clothing: at bed time put on your best lingerie. Don't stop calling him darling, honey, baby or even big daddy; don't stop calling her sweet heart, sexy lady, beautiful, sweetie; this keeps the fire burning even after many years of marriage. Say the magic word tell your partner how attractive they look and how fine they are, this keep the blaze going. Words are so powerful! You can build your spouse up are tear them down with negative words, speak peace and life over your spouse.

Make sure you give each other time to miss one another, let your spouse have their own time alone. Give them some space to enjoy alone, some me time. Whatever you do make sure you have time for sexual Intimacy and if you are not able to have intercourse be romantic. Keep romance alive in your marriage it shouldn't ever get boring it should always be excited; you got to work at it. Don't let old routines set in, avoid being boring: every weekend do something together, even if you have children hire a baby sitter, go out on a dinner date or to the movies or check into a hotel to enjoy each other for a few hours.

Sometimes you have to spice things up after being in a long time relationship, keep it interesting. You have to be willing to try new things together, it'll make all the difference, I promise. Have lots of sex after all it's a gift from God. Research shows that the more a couple connects sexually, the more they want to experience it with one another, Real talk! Couples must make it a priority to keep the spark ignited, never let the flames go out. Surprise your partner from time to time with a love note, card telling them how much they mean to you. Ladies surprise your hubby with an extra special dinner. Men's surprise your sweet heart with a dozen of roses every now and then.

Do something that you both enjoy doing together to keep the spark alive. Give your best when making love, don't half step. If you expect to be loved, then you need to give your best. Keep love alive by giving each other a massage; send a sweet text, anything that's exciting to arouse your partner. Don't wait until valentines to say I love you; tell your spouse every day that you love them. Say thanks for the little things your partner do for you. Set aside time every night; even if you both just lie in bed together and engage in an enjoyable conversation. Make your spouse feel valued and wanted. Let the fire continue to burn between you and the love of your life. No matter what, don't let nothing or nobody put out your fire. Keep the fire Burning!

Say I Love You:

Each time you tell your spouse how much you love them, this strengthens your relationship. Your spouse should always be reminded of how much you love them. Shout it out loud that you love them even if someone is around. Don't be ashamed to say I love you. Love is deep and it needs to be heard. Love never fails, it works no evil. Even when you and your spouse have a misunderstanding, the love that you have for one another should conquer that very thing. Love is everlasting, no matter what!

Chapter 6

Intimacy

Most times in a marriage, sex and intimacy are topics that prove to be one of the major hardships in some relationships. A healthy sexual life is so important it's like oxygen. It's one way of knowing that your relationship is headed in the right direction. Your bedroom should be a special place where you and your spouse can relax, reconnect, re-energize, and enjoy one another. My spouse and I have always kept our bedroom a very special place where we can enjoy. Your bedroom should be a place to celebrate your union, with no interference from the world. My priority was always to keep our bedroom a special place to celebrate our marriage.

God should be your number one priority, second your spouse; your spouse should be greatly loved by showing how much you care for each other. Make your room *a sanctuary of bliss for your union*. You need to celebrate and reunite with your partner every chance you get. I challenge you to *celebrate* your union and stay on your *honeymoon*! Being married, you must understand that it's important to learn how valuable unity is to a husband and wife. Whatever you do, please don't take your marriage for granted. When you lose the importance of being one, enjoy your spouse to the fullest. No matter what, it's for the glory of God to be seen as both of you continue to celebrate this great union.

If your marriage is built upon the love of Christ, then both of you will enjoy more than the physical part. When it comes down to sex, could it be that some of you enjoy sex less when husband or wife only wants the physical part? But what if it's emotional, are even spiritual for them? And what's even better is the implications of having a deeper than physical connection with your spouse in your bedroom. The truth of the matter is that sex is incredibly enjoyable. Our Creator has blessed a husband and a wife with sex as a miraculous blessing!

As one of the deepest acts of love shared between two people, making them one is awesome. One body, one heart, one love equals passionate pleasure. What a joy intimacy becomes when both become "one flesh." Read the Song of Solomon and see for yourself what has been written about love. God didn't just make sex enjoyable just for the man or for the woman, he made it for both spouses to be a *mind-blowing pleasure* for each other. Sex is one of the greatest human experiences. It is or should be a great experience for the soul spirit and nature. Sex has a possibility to be an encounter where the normal boundaries of self are broken down, where what you feel can be encountered, without change or loss of strength and power, by another. Sex is the closet human identical to communication of one soul to another. Sex requires a willingness to explore not only for pleasure, but for intimacy as well. For instance, as long as sex is about your pleasure and not about you and your partner, this can become an issue in pursuing real intimacy. Without intimacy and trust, sex is likely to be void of feelings, which is an essential dimension of pleasure that is felt.

We are one in God's sight when we marry, never to be separated. However, we are also to build oneness into our marriage. The "one flesh" relationship is obviously physical, involving the sexual relationship—but it is more than that. It includes intimacy between a husband and wife in every way—physically, spiritually, and emotionally. We as women long for intimacy with our husbands. Some men are not good about spiritual or emotional intimacy but seem to desire only physical intimacy. If this is so, perhaps you need to work on communicating your need for other kinds of intimacy with your spouse. Just remember that we do live in a fallen world and you may never have the kind of intimacy with your husband that you desire. Instead of letting that create dissatisfaction with your mate, let it draw you nearer to Christ, who wants to give you the type of intimacy you desire.

1 Corinthians 7:1-9 "Now for the matters you wrote about: It is good for a man not to have sexual relations with a woman." ² But since sexual immorality is occurring, each man should have sexual relations with his own wife, and each woman with her own husband. ³ The husband should fulfill his marital duty to his wife, and likewise the wife to her husband. ⁴ The wife does not have authority over her own body but yields it to her husband. In the same way, the husband does not have authority over his own body but yields it to his wife. ⁵ Do not deprive each other except perhaps by mutual consent and for a time, so that you may devote yourselves to prayer. Then come together again so that Satan will not tempt you because of your lack of self-control. ⁶ I say this as a concession, not as a command. ⁷ I wish that all of you were as I am. But each of you has your own gift from God; one has this gift, another has that. ⁸ Now to the unmarried[a] and the widows I say: It is good for them to stay unmarried, as I do. ⁹ But if they cannot control themselves, they should marry, for it is better to marry than to burn with passion.

Know that when we marry, we are no longer to retain our rights over our own bodies but are to give that authority to our spouse. Remember that two has become one now; your husband is part of you, not separate. When he need you physically, you are to meet his needs. You have died and are to live for Christ who expects you to take care of one another's needs. There are many marriages that could have been saved if the wife had understood that her body belongs to her husband, not for abuse, but for fulfilling his sexual needs.

Marriage pictures the relationship between Christ and his church's oneness in covenant comes with our entry into covenant with him, and oneness sexually should only come with commitment in a marriage. When sex takes place before marriage, it breaks the picture of the covenant and commitment we have with Christ. Adultery does the same thing. I have often heard it said that sins are all the same before God. The Bible tells and encourages all of us as wives to adopt a very important principle. Do not refuse sex with your husband unless you really have a physical reason, or other good reasons. If at all possible, say yes! This will result in a much happier man. Personally I will say that I have found this to be true—my husband is much more fun and less grouchy (hello)! Men and women are wired very differently. When women are tired they want to go sleep; when men are tired or exhausted, they want sex. Sex is their way of unwinding, no matter how tired they are, physically or mentally! Men's sexuality is part of their identity and extremely important to their masculinity to be rejected, sexually is taken personally! The word of God tells us that your body is not your own, nor his body his own—we belong to each other.

According to 1 Corinthians 7:1-9, are you willing to give yourself to your husband sexually without considering your own desires or needs? Are you prepared to give him the authority over your body? If you are not, you are in sin, disobeying God's direct command and his principle of oneness, and you are putting your marriage at risk. If you have been disobedient in this area, take time to confess this to God and to your husband and ask for forgiveness. This is not to be taken lightly because this is God's design for your marriage. He is the designer and God knows exactly what works best for your marriage, ask God for grace to die to self in this area and put the needs of your spouse before your own.

I believe that marriage and children are ways that God deals with our sinful selfishness, making us more like Jesus, whose unselfishness resulted in our salvation. If we follow God's marriage principles, we become more Christlike. One of the differences between husbands and wives is illustrated by their attitudes toward sex when they are physically tired. Sex is usually the last thing a wife wants when she's tired, but it provides her husband the relaxation he needs for restoring sleep. Some men prefer sex at night while some men prefer to begin the day with this grafting experience. Another difference is that after a quarrel, a woman looks for words of reconciliation but a man often looks for sex to heal the breach and restore oneness with his wife. Someone stated the difference this way:

"A man gives love for sex, a woman gives sex for love. This validates the idea that men seek intimacy through sex. That is why they want to have sex when there has been an argument. This may be your husband's attempts to console you by suggesting sex when you are hurting for some reason. A wife may demonstrate her love in innumerable other ways, but it is often negated by her rejections or lack of enjoyment of sex. To a man, sex is the most meaningful demonstration of love and self-worth. A husband's gift of sexual pleasure is full of meaning.

Marital intimacy can open your relationship to a whole new level of enjoyment and closeness. It is important, however, to remember that intimacy does not always mean sexuality. An often forgotten aspect of intimacy is emotional and physical intimacy and when one of the other is most appropriate. Offering your spouse one type when they really need the other can create problems in your relationship. I truly believe that sex is a great gift from God.

Intimacy is not always physical; intimacy is more than just a physical connection. It comes from forming a deep connection with another person. It's about knowing their hopes, goals, fears, and what makes them the way they are. In this type of relationship, sexual intimacy goes hand in hand, as one builds the other. Sometimes, deep intimacy can come without words. It may be a glance as you drive along the highway, and you appreciate the view together, or along in the park, holding hands.

Physical intimacy, on the other hand, does not mean sex. Women generally like to start with hugging, kissing, and other forms of physical intimacy before sex begins. Men also enjoy these things; however, to feel connected to their spouse men usually need sex too. Men and women are really looking for the same thing. It is their approach that differs. We feel connected, we all feel connected. Women place more importance on the emotional connection and men on the physical, but both are required by everyone.

Intimacy is one of the most important things in a relationship. Understanding how to meet your spouse's needs is the first step in building a strong, long lasting relationship that both of you will be happy with. Lack of intimacy in a marriage is a major issue, something you should confront as soon as possible. If you don't address an intimacy problem, it could form a serious fissure in your relationship and lead you and your loved one to an unhappy marriage or a divorce. Coping with intimacy issues in a marriage is difficult but not impossible work. Intimacy can only be created through honest communication. This doesn't mean that you should start wagging your fingers in your spouse's face. This is a partnership; you're each other fault and each is charged with doing the work necessary to keep romance and love alive in a marriage. When you talk to your partner, be sure to take a balance and to provide solutions. Don't back your loved one in a corner later: If you constantly criticize or blame your spouse, he or she may deny there's a problem or even they may walk out.

Chapter 7

Don't Let the Devil Steal Your Marriage

Satan comes to do three things: steal, kill, and destroy your marriage. Notice anything that God has joined together, Satan tries hard to destroy it. He wants to destroy every good relationship. Why? Because he loves conflicts and arguments. He wants to cause confusion, arguments, stress, hurt, disappointment, anger, and chaos. He loves to do it. The book of James tells us, you need give it to God and let him have control. Then you have to do some defensive action. You have to resist the devil and realize what he's doing. Don't be unaware of Satan's schemes. In other words, wise up and recognize Satan's tactics.

Satan wants to make you think that your spouse has been cheating on you, that he or she been seeking to sleeping around with another man or woman. Stay alert, keep your eyes on the Lord, because

Satan is *sneaky*. He will catch you off guard when you least expect it. Please keep your marriage relationship "in the Lord" just as you tried to keep a good testimony outside of the home. Stay close to the Lord; in the matter of your marriage, go to God in prayer and tell him all about it.

Don't let Satan's lies get into your thinking. Be on guard against negative thoughts about your spouse. Take such thoughts to the Lord and release them. In a marriage, you need to have faith because God sees a lot of things from above that you cannot see where you are. Have faith; he knows what he's doing. Trust him; stand strong in faith and don't listen to your emotions because they will lie to you. It doesn't matter what it feels like or seems like at the time, God will heal if you are having or have challenges in your marriage. Let go and let God; he's able to bring about a change.

Satan is always out to destroy your marriage. Pray for your spouse. When a spouse has broken his covenant promise, he has been deceived by the enemy. What therefore God has joined together let no man put asunder. Know how Satan operates, by studying the word of God. How does he operate? He doesn't stand around with a pitch folk at all and a red suit. He plays on your pride, particularly wounded pride. He tells you what he wants you to hear. He whispers in your ear and gives you little thoughts, suggestions, and ideas.

When you're in the middle of an argument, he starts whispering things in your ear, like "You don't have to take this kind of stuff retaliate. Who do they think they are? Get even, assert yourself. Don't put up with this kind of mess. Show 'em who's boss." He tells you all the things your pride would love to hear. In response, you have to say, "Satan I know that's you." Resist him in the name of Jesus and he has to flee. You resist the devil the same way Jesus did. He quoted scriptures. Memorize Proverbs 13:10: "pride leads to conflicts." The next time you get into an argument, the Lord will bring the verse to mind. Stop and ask yourself, how am I being pride here? What am I not willing to admit? Why am I not willing to compromise? There is a great promise in James 4:7, "Submit yourselves to God. Resist the devil, and he will flee from you." You don't have to put up with him. Give in to God and get wise to Satan's schemes.

According to the Bible, Satan prowls around like a lion looking for someone to devour (1 Peter 5:8), but many times he probably doesn't have to do that much, if Satan can get you to lie (Colossians 3:9) to your spouse. Lying can destroy trust in a marriage.

There are too many Christian marriages ending up in divorce. I know this Christian couple who was married for forty years. They have allowed the enemy to come in and destroy their union, and they are both ministers of the gospel. Something in this marriage was lacking, maybe the lack of quality time, lack of commitment, or it may even be because of the devil himself. Making time for one another is incredibly important.

Everyday life is busy as everyone knows. It can be difficult to make time for things, even when there are things you want to do. The same is true when trying to make time for your spouse. A good way to make time for one another is to plan a date night, go out to dinner to the movies, whatever you and your spouse decide to do. Spending this time is a great way to rekindle your love life. In order to keep your love alive in your marriage, it's important that the affection still be present in the relationship. Even small forms of affections like a regular morning kiss or an addition of a little daily flirting will take your relationship to new heights. These small signs of love mean much more than the actual actions itself. It means the love is not gone. To make your spouse feel even more special and loved, it's a good idea to participate in small acts of kindness that your partner will appreciate. It will make the person you love feel important to you. It will show them how much you care about their needs and desires.

Feeling appreciated makes one feel closer to one another and feeling closer to your spouse is the first step toward keeping your love strong for as long as you are together. It's important in every marriage to maintain communication. This communication is not just limited to the big things in your partner's life. Engage in meaningful conversation open communication will keep yourselves up dated with each other's lives and you'll know how he/she feels about your relationship. Please don't forget to tell each other that you love one another. Every time you say I love you and mean it your marriage is strengthen. It may seem like a little small thing but it is very important in maintaining a healthy relationship with your spouse. Marriage is a long road that has its ups and downs.

The devil will come to you when you are having difficulties in your marriage and tell you things like there is no hope for your marriage. It can't be saved this may be the most devasting lie of all. Because with God all things are possible in a dying marriage, he just need two willing parties. God knows how to get you out of the mess you get yourselves into. God is God of restoration; he can restore any dead situation. If you began to think there is no hope for your marriage, realize that, with God all things are possible. God can fix anything.

Satan will try his best to destroy your marriage, he will slip in any way that he can, he'll come through family members, friends even through your children, he will come in to whisper negative and evil thoughts to you about your spouse. Stay prayed up and keep your heart guarded with truth, put God first in your marriage and keep everybody else out, whatever you do, don't allow the third party into your union. The enemy hates God and he hates marriages, because marriages itself is portrayal of the Gospel (Ephesians 5:32).

The Devil wants to do whatever he can do to undermine marriages. One of the devils most effective strategies is to corrupt the Gospel portrayal union of a marriage to attack couples before they say "I Do" through sexual sin. What follows are several of Satan's most common plots to attacking marriage before the very beginning. What the enemy tries to do is make a pattern of obeying our desires instead of Gods directions. God's way are the right way, Satan himself wants us to believe they are not.

Satan goal is for us to develop a consistence pattern of resisting the spirit of God and follow our sinful desires once we get into marriage. What he really want us to learn to resist service and pursue selfishness. Most times if we learn what we want to do before getting married, will carry that same spirit into the days that follow our wedding this can become very dangerous because service and sacrifice is essential to a healthy, honoring marriage. In a marriage love is shown by many daily decisions to wash the dishes, or to cook dinner even when you don't feel like it, love covers a multitude of things.

If your relationship before you marry is characterized by given into urges of the immediate desire, you'll likely struggle when you get into the nitty-gritty of marriage life. The enemy loves insecure in a marriage; my husband and I always had a positive reason to be faithful to each other. Being able to trust your spouse causes your marriage to be healthy. Insecure is a bad spirit, don't allow the enemy to defeat your marriage with this spirit.

The devil is the enemy. Satan doesn't want your marriage to survive. One thing the devil doesn't want your marriage to do is to make an impact for God's kingdom. Your spouse and you are teammates in a war against the enemy. All the devil desires to do, is to destroy what God has joined together. He will try any way he can to destroy your union. You and your partner are in this union together, not to be enemies against one another. Yes, there's going to be times in your marriage when you may have some disagreements; you may not see eye to eye in every situation. The devil may try to make you feel that your spouse is fighting against you. The devil is a liar and the truth is not in him. Your spouse is not your enemy, no matter what you and your spouse faces, no matter how tough your struggles get, no matter what your spouse does or do not do, your partner is not your enemy.

It's so important to know Satan's devices; this will help you recognize the enemy when he tries to attack your marriage. When the enemy tries to get you upset and angry when disagreement takes place, don't focus on all the negatives because this will get you and your spouse nowhere except to become angry, frustrated, and hurt. Give it to the Lord in prayer. When you submit yourself to God, the Bible tells us that we can resist the devil and he will flee. Pray and ask God to preserve, protect, strengthen, and keep your marriage.

Anytime you declare Christ over your marriage, the enemy hates you. All the devil desires to do is to sift your marriage as wheat.

By any chance the devil wants to test your loyalty and tempt you! He will try everything in his power to tempt you and to make you stumble and fall! That's why it's necessary to be always ready by keeping your armor on. Instead of becoming a victim, rise up and become a victor. And laugh at the enemy in the face. Prepare yourselves for attacks to happen, stay prayed up, and know that God is Lord over your marriage. Praise God for his unfailing power that gives you and your spouse the victory to overcome the stumbling blocks in your lives and over your marriage.

Biography

Sandra Wilson was born in Walkerton Virginia, to the late Mr. Rueben and Mrs. Marian Gaines, she has five siblings. She's married to an awesome man of God Larry Wilson sr, for twenty nine years, a total of thirty five blessed years, since this union the Lord has blessed them with nine children, seventeen grand's, and four beautiful daughter-in-laws. She's been a professional house wife, for twenty five years. She's an Evangelist; she enjoys Preaching the Gospel Truth, and enjoys serving others. She's the President over the Help ministry, she serve in the Outreach Ministry, at Berachah Fellowship Church where Pastor Ronald & Deidra Smith is Founders. She and her family have been attending this great Ministry for eleven years. In 2012 she received her bachelor's degree in psychology, from Troy University. She's preparing to go back to College to receive her Master's in psychology, to become a Certified Counselor. During her spare time she enjoys decorating, sewing, painting, and making bless pillows to give away. She believes that she was created with a purpose, to discover a place which surpasses all understanding through Jesus Christ our Lord. She's living out her faith which is backed up by the Holy Spirit. She's happily choosing to be her husband's helper because faith powers every decision she makes. She has always desired to be a great wife and to be dedicated to serving her family.

NOTES

NOTES

NOTES

NOTES

NOTES

NOTES

NOTES

NOTES

NOTES

NOTES

NOTES

CPSIA information can be obtained at www.ICGtesting.com
Printed in the USA
BVOW08s1001130616

451819BV00001B/15/P